SOUL TALK

JOURNAL

Kirk Byron Jones

Introduction

Showing Your Soul to Yourself: Chronicling Your Soul Talk

I have journaled since leaving my first pastorate in 1984. Founding and leading Beacon Light Baptist Church in my home of New Orleans, LA was so exciting and fulfilling that I wanted to make sure I remembered as much of it, especially the marvelous persons, as possible. My journaling practice expanded over the years, as I began to appreciate how much it helped to keep me awake to my life, and aware and appreciative. More than helping me to stay in the know about my life, journaling helps me to stay in charge of my life. Deliberately recording experiences and explorations that matter makes me more deliberate about not just responding to life, but intentionally and thoughtfully creating life. I now maintain several journals, one exclusively devoted to my soul talk dialogue. Journaling helps me to show my soul to myself.

Whether you choose to use the *Soul Talk Journal* or not, I strongly encourage you to take some moments to record highlights from your soul talk sessions. My habit is to jot a word or phrase during the session itself. Often but not always, I then take a moment to summarize my messages, images, ideas, and impressions that may have surfaced during the session. Doing so helps me to stay alert for recurring themes. Also, it is important for me to note guidance that I am led to put into practice.

Here are three tips for you to consider. First, experiment sometimes writing with your non-dominate hand. Most of us have less control over our non-dominate hand when writing. This can lead to writing that is not over-thought and less contrived. Your unconscious may be more easily expressed when you are using your other hand for writing, releasing matter hidden or suppressed inside you. Second, pay careful attention to writing that surprises you in some way. Notice what seems to be written through you. Ponder what you wrote, but had not intended to write. This is what the beloved Howard Thurman referred to as "the growing edge." Third, don't just write, doodle. Let yourself sketch images as well as write words. Sometimes the soul can say in an image what you may need hundreds of words to express.

Soul Talk Journal pages are formatted for you to write something of importance during any one or all of the 7 soul talk steps. Don't feel pressed to fill the page with words. If a single page is not enough, use more than one page for a single session's entry.

Remember, when journaling the main goal is to honestly record your thoughts and feelings. Make a habit of rereading entries to spot recurring soul messages and track progress on goals inspired by dialogue with your soul.

For Anne Morrow Lindbergh, chronicling living enlivened living: *I must write it all out at any cost. Writing is thinking. It is more than living, for me it is conscious living.*

Hopefully, if it is not already, journaling will become for you *a soul-growth necessity.* (Excerpted from *Soul Talk: How to Have the Most Important Conversation of All*)

Journal Pages

Journal Entry

Date : _____   Time : _____

Stillness

_____

_____

_____

Release

_____

_____

_____

Deep Listening

_____

_____

_____

Staying

_____

_____

_____

Honesty

_____

_____

_____

Gentleness

_____

_____

_____

New Truth Breakthrough

_____

_____

_____

Journal Entry

Date : _____   Time : _____

Stillness

_____

_____

_____

Release

_____

_____

_____

Deep Listening

_____

_____

_____

Staying

_____

_____

_____

Honesty

_____

_____

_____

Gentleness

_____

_____

_____

New Truth Breakthrough

_____

_____

_____

Journal Entry

Date : _____   Time : _____

Stillness

_____

_____

_____

Release

_____

_____

_____

Deep Listening

_____

_____

_____

Staying

_____

_____

_____

Honesty

_____

_____

_____

Gentleness

_____

_____

_____

New Truth Breakthrough

_____

_____

_____

Journal Entry

Date : _____   Time : _____

Stillness

_____

_____

_____

Release

_____

_____

_____

Deep Listening

_____

_____

_____

Staying

_____

_____

_____

Honesty

_____

_____

_____

Gentleness

_____

_____

_____

New Truth Breakthrough

_____

_____

_____

Journal Entry

Date : _____   Time : _____

Stillness

_____

_____

_____

Release

_____

_____

_____

Deep Listening

_____

_____

_____

Staying

_____

_____

_____

Honesty

_____

_____

_____

Gentleness

_____

_____

_____

New Truth Breakthrough

_____

_____

_____

Journal Entry

Date : _____   Time : _____

Stillness

_____

_____

_____

Release

_____

_____

_____

Deep Listening

_____

_____

_____

Staying

_____

_____

_____

Honesty

_____

_____

_____

Gentleness

_____

_____

_____

New Truth Breakthrough

_____

_____

_____

Journal Entry

Date : _____   Time : _____

Stillness

_____

_____

_____

Release

_____

_____

_____

Deep Listening

_____

_____

_____

Staying

_____

_____

_____

Honesty

_____

_____

_____

Gentleness

_____

_____

_____

New Truth Breakthrough

_____

_____

_____

Journal Entry

Date : _____   Time : _____

Stillness

_____

_____

_____

Release

_____

_____

_____

Deep Listening

_____

_____

_____

Staying

_____

_____

_____

Honesty

_____

_____

_____

Gentleness

_____

_____

_____

New Truth Breakthrough

_____

_____

_____

Journal Entry

Date : _____   Time : _____

Stillness

_____

_____

_____

Release

_____

_____

_____

Deep Listening

_____

_____

_____

Staying

_____

_____

_____

Honesty

_____

_____

_____

Gentleness

_____

_____

_____

New Truth Breakthrough

_____

_____

_____

Journal Entry

Date : _____   Time : _____

Stillness

_____

_____

_____

Release

_____

_____

_____

Deep Listening

_____

_____

_____

Staying

_____

_____

_____

Honesty

_____

_____

_____

Gentleness

_____

_____

_____

New Truth Breakthrough

_____

_____

_____

Journal Entry

Date : _____   Time : _____

Stillness

_____

_____

_____

Release

_____

_____

_____

Deep Listening

_____

_____

_____

Staying

_____

_____

_____

Honesty

_____

_____

_____

Gentleness

_____

_____

_____

New Truth Breakthrough

_____

_____

_____

Journal Entry

Date : _____   Time : _____

Stillness

_____

_____

_____

Release

_____

_____

_____

Deep Listening

_____

_____

_____

Staying

_____

_____

_____

Honesty

_____

_____

_____

Gentleness

_____

_____

_____

New Truth Breakthrough

_____

_____

_____

Journal Entry

Date : _____   Time : _____

Stillness

_____

_____

_____

Release

_____

_____

_____

Deep Listening

_____

_____

_____

Staying

_____

_____

_____

Honesty

_____

_____

_____

Gentleness

_____

_____

_____

New Truth Breakthrough

_____

_____

_____

Journal Entry

Date : _____   Time : _____

Stillness

_____

_____

_____

Release

_____

_____

_____

Deep Listening

_____

_____

_____

Staying

_____

_____

_____

Honesty

_____

_____

_____

Gentleness

_____

_____

_____

New Truth Breakthrough

_____

_____

_____

Journal Entry

Date : _____   Time : _____

Stillness

_____

_____

_____

Release

_____

_____

_____

Deep Listening

_____

_____

_____

Staying

_____

_____

_____

Honesty

_____

_____

_____

Gentleness

_____

_____

_____

New Truth Breakthrough

_____

_____

_____

Journal Entry

Date : _____   Time : _____

Stillness

_____
_____
_____

Release

_____
_____
_____

Deep Listening

_____
_____
_____

Staying

_____
_____
_____

Honesty

_____
_____
_____

Gentleness

_____
_____
_____

New Truth Breakthrough

_____
_____
_____

Journal Entry

Date : _____   Time : _____

Stillness

_____
_____
_____

Release

_____
_____
_____

Deep Listening

_____
_____
_____

Staying

_____
_____
_____

Honesty

_____
_____
_____

Gentleness

_____
_____
_____

New Truth Breakthrough

_____
_____
_____

Journal Entry

Date : _____   Time : _____

Stillness

_____

_____

_____

Release

_____

_____

_____

Deep Listening

_____

_____

_____

Staying

_____

_____

_____

Honesty

_____

_____

_____

Gentleness

_____

_____

_____

New Truth Breakthrough

_____

_____

_____

Journal Entry

Date : _____ Time : _____

Stillness

_____
_____
_____

Release

_____
_____
_____

Deep Listening

_____
_____
_____

Staying

_____
_____
_____

Honesty

_____
_____
_____

Gentleness

_____
_____
_____

New Truth Breakthrough

_____
_____
_____

Journal Entry

Date : _____   Time : _____

Stillness

_____

_____

_____

Release

_____

_____

_____

Deep Listening

_____

_____

_____

Staying

_____

_____

_____

Honesty

_____

_____

_____

Gentleness

_____

_____

_____

New Truth Breakthrough

_____

_____

_____

Journal Entry

Date : _____   Time : _____

Stillness

_____

_____

_____

Release

_____

_____

_____

Deep Listening

_____

_____

_____

Staying

_____

_____

_____

Honesty

_____

_____

_____

Gentleness

_____

_____

_____

New Truth Breakthrough

_____

_____

_____

Journal Entry

Date : _____   Time : _____

Stillness

_____

_____

_____

Release

_____

_____

_____

Deep Listening

_____

_____

_____

Staying

_____

_____

_____

Honesty

_____

_____

_____

Gentleness

_____

_____

_____

New Truth Breakthrough

_____

_____

_____

Journal Entry

Date : _____   Time : _____

Stillness

_____
_____
_____

Release

_____
_____
_____

Deep Listening

_____
_____
_____

Staying

_____
_____
_____

Honesty

_____
_____
_____

Gentleness

_____
_____
_____

New Truth Breakthrough

_____
_____
_____

Journal Entry

Date : _____   Time : _____

Stillness

_____

_____

_____

Release

_____

_____

_____

Deep Listening

_____

_____

_____

Staying

_____

_____

_____

Honesty

_____

_____

_____

Gentleness

_____

_____

_____

New Truth Breakthrough

_____

_____

_____

Journal Entry

Date : _____   Time : _____

Stillness

_____

_____

_____

Release

_____

_____

_____

Deep Listening

_____

_____

_____

Staying

_____

_____

_____

Honesty

_____

_____

_____

Gentleness

_____

_____

_____

New Truth Breakthrough

_____

_____

_____

Journal Entry

Date : _____ Time : _____

Stillness

_____

_____

_____

Release

_____

_____

_____

Deep Listening

_____

_____

_____

Staying

_____

_____

_____

Honesty

_____

_____

_____

Gentleness

_____

_____

_____

New Truth Breakthrough

_____

_____

_____

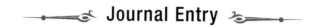 Journal Entry

Date : _____   Time : _____

Stillness

_____

_____

_____

Release

_____

_____

_____

Deep Listening

_____

_____

_____

Staying

_____

_____

_____

Honesty

_____

_____

_____

Gentleness

_____

_____

_____

New Truth Breakthrough

_____

_____

_____

Journal Entry

Date : _____   Time : _____

Stillness

_____
_____
_____

Release

_____
_____
_____

Deep Listening

_____
_____
_____

Staying

_____
_____
_____

Honesty

_____
_____
_____

Gentleness

_____
_____
_____

New Truth Breakthrough

_____
_____
_____

Journal Entry

Date : _____ Time : _____

Stillness

_____

_____

_____

Release

_____

_____

_____

Deep Listening

_____

_____

_____

Staying

_____

_____

_____

Honesty

_____

_____

_____

Gentleness

_____

_____

_____

New Truth Breakthrough

_____

_____

_____

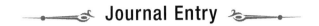# Journal Entry

Date : _____   Time : _____

Stillness

_____

_____

_____

Release

_____

_____

_____

Deep Listening

_____

_____

_____

Staying

_____

_____

_____

Honesty

_____

_____

_____

Gentleness

_____

_____

_____

New Truth Breakthrough

_____

_____

_____

Journal Entry

Date : _____   Time : _____

Stillness

_____

_____

_____

Release

_____

_____

_____

Deep Listening

_____

_____

_____

Staying

_____

_____

_____

Honesty

_____

_____

_____

Gentleness

_____

_____

_____

New Truth Breakthrough

_____

_____

_____

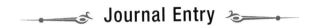 Journal Entry

Date : _____   Time : _____

Stillness

_____

_____

_____

Release

_____

_____

_____

Deep Listening

_____

_____

_____

Staying

_____

_____

_____

Honesty

_____

_____

_____

Gentleness

_____

_____

_____

New Truth Breakthrough

_____

_____

_____

Journal Entry

Date : _____   Time : _____

Stillness

_____

_____

_____

Release

_____

_____

_____

Deep Listening

_____

_____

_____

Staying

_____

_____

_____

Honesty

_____

_____

_____

Gentleness

_____

_____

_____

New Truth Breakthrough

_____

_____

_____

Journal Entry

Date : _____   Time : _____

Stillness

_____
_____
_____

Release

_____
_____
_____

Deep Listening

_____
_____
_____

Staying

_____
_____
_____

Honesty

_____
_____
_____

Gentleness

_____
_____
_____

New Truth Breakthrough

_____
_____
_____

Journal Entry

Date : _____   Time : _____

Stillness

_____
_____
_____

Release

_____
_____
_____

Deep Listening

_____
_____
_____

Staying

_____
_____
_____

Honesty

_____
_____
_____

Gentleness

_____
_____
_____

New Truth Breakthrough

_____
_____
_____

Journal Entry

Date : _____   Time : _____

Stillness

_____
_____
_____

Release

_____
_____
_____

Deep Listening

_____
_____
_____

Staying

_____
_____
_____

Honesty

_____
_____
_____

Gentleness

_____
_____
_____

New Truth Breakthrough

_____
_____
_____

Journal Entry

Date : _____   Time : _____

Stillness

_____

_____

_____

Release

_____

_____

_____

Deep Listening

_____

_____

_____

Staying

_____

_____

_____

Honesty

_____

_____

_____

Gentleness

_____

_____

_____

New Truth Breakthrough

_____

_____

_____

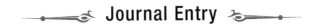# Journal Entry

Date : _____   Time : _____

Stillness

_____
_____
_____

Release

_____
_____
_____

Deep Listening

_____
_____
_____

Staying

_____
_____
_____

Honesty

_____
_____
_____

Gentleness

_____
_____
_____

New Truth Breakthrough

_____
_____
_____

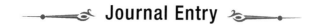 Journal Entry

Date : _____   Time : _____

Stillness

_____

_____

_____

Release

_____

_____

_____

Deep Listening

_____

_____

_____

Staying

_____

_____

_____

Honesty

_____

_____

_____

Gentleness

_____

_____

_____

New Truth Breakthrough

_____

_____

_____

Journal Entry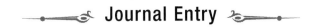

Date : _____   Time : _____

Stillness

_____

_____

_____

Release

_____

_____

_____

Deep Listening

_____

_____

_____

Staying

_____

_____

_____

Honesty

_____

_____

_____

Gentleness

_____

_____

_____

New Truth Breakthrough

_____

_____

_____

Journal Entry

Date : _____   Time : _____

Stillness

_____

_____

_____

Release

_____

_____

_____

Deep Listening

_____

_____

_____

Staying

_____

_____

_____

Honesty

_____

_____

_____

Gentleness

_____

_____

_____

New Truth Breakthrough

_____

_____

_____

Journal Entry

Date : _____   Time : _____

Stillness

_____
_____
_____

Release

_____
_____
_____

Deep Listening

_____
_____
_____

Staying

_____
_____
_____

Honesty

_____
_____
_____

Gentleness

_____
_____
_____

New Truth Breakthrough

_____
_____
_____

Journal Entry

Date : _____   Time : _____

Stillness

_____

_____

_____

Release

_____

_____

_____

Deep Listening

_____

_____

_____

Staying

_____

_____

_____

Honesty

_____

_____

_____

Gentleness

_____

_____

_____

New Truth Breakthrough

_____

_____

_____

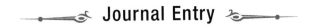

Journal Entry

Date : _____   Time : _____

Stillness

_____
_____
_____

Release

_____
_____
_____

Deep Listening

_____
_____
_____

Staying

_____
_____
_____

Honesty

_____
_____
_____

Gentleness

_____
_____
_____

New Truth Breakthrough

_____
_____
_____

Journal Entry

Date : _____   Time : _____

Stillness

_____

_____

_____

Release

_____

_____

_____

Deep Listening

_____

_____

_____

Staying

_____

_____

_____

Honesty

_____

_____

_____

Gentleness

_____

_____

_____

New Truth Breakthrough

_____

_____

_____

Journal Entry

Date : _____   Time : _____

Stillness

_____
_____
_____

Release

_____
_____
_____

Deep Listening

_____
_____
_____

Staying

_____
_____
_____

Honesty

_____
_____
_____

Gentleness

_____
_____
_____

New Truth Breakthrough

_____
_____
_____

Journal Entry

Date : _____   Time : _____

Stillness

_____

_____

_____

Release

_____

_____

_____

Deep Listening

_____

_____

_____

Staying

_____

_____

_____

Honesty

_____

_____

_____

Gentleness

_____

_____

_____

New Truth Breakthrough

_____

_____

_____

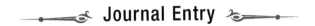# Journal Entry

Date : _____   Time : _____

Stillness

_____

_____

_____

Release

_____

_____

_____

Deep Listening

_____

_____

_____

Staying

_____

_____

_____

Honesty

_____

_____

_____

Gentleness

_____

_____

_____

New Truth Breakthrough

_____

_____

_____

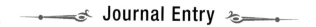 Journal Entry

Date : _____   Time : _____

Stillness

_____
_____
_____

Release

_____
_____
_____

Deep Listening

_____
_____
_____

Staying

_____
_____
_____

Honesty

_____
_____
_____

Gentleness

_____
_____
_____

New Truth Breakthrough

_____
_____
_____

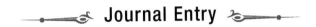 **Journal Entry**

Date : _____   Time : _____

Stillness

_____
_____
_____

Release

_____
_____
_____

Deep Listening

_____
_____
_____

Staying

_____
_____
_____

Honesty

_____
_____
_____

Gentleness

_____
_____
_____

New Truth Breakthrough

_____
_____
_____

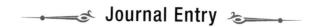# Journal Entry

Date : _____   Time : _____

Stillness

_____
_____
_____

Release

_____
_____
_____

Deep Listening

_____
_____
_____

Staying

_____
_____
_____

Honesty

_____
_____
_____

Gentleness

_____
_____
_____

New Truth Breakthrough

_____
_____
_____

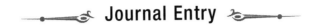 Journal Entry

Date : _____   Time : _____

Stillness

_____
_____
_____

Release

_____
_____
_____

Deep Listening

_____
_____
_____

Staying

_____
_____
_____

Honesty

_____
_____
_____

Gentleness

_____
_____
_____

New Truth Breakthrough

_____
_____
_____

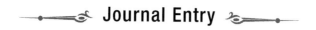 **Journal Entry**

Date : _____   Time : _____

Stillness

_____

_____

_____

Release

_____

_____

_____

Deep Listening

_____

_____

_____

Staying

_____

_____

_____

Honesty

_____

_____

_____

Gentleness

_____

_____

_____

New Truth Breakthrough

_____

_____

_____

Journal Entry

Date : _____   Time : _____

Stillness

_____
_____
_____

Release

_____
_____
_____

Deep Listening

_____
_____
_____

Staying

_____
_____
_____

Honesty

_____
_____
_____

Gentleness

_____
_____
_____

New Truth Breakthrough

_____
_____
_____

Journal Entry

Date : _____   Time : _____

Stillness

_____

_____

_____

Release

_____

_____

_____

Deep Listening

_____

_____

_____

Staying

_____

_____

_____

Honesty

_____

_____

_____

Gentleness

_____

_____

_____

New Truth Breakthrough

_____

_____

_____

Journal Entry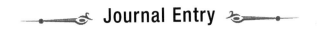

Date : _____   Time : _____

Stillness

_____

_____

_____

Release

_____

_____

_____

Deep Listening

_____

_____

_____

Staying

_____

_____

_____

Honesty

_____

_____

_____

Gentleness

_____

_____

_____

New Truth Breakthrough

_____

_____

_____

Journal Entry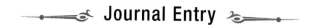

Date : _____   Time : _____

Stillness

_____

_____

_____

Release

_____

_____

_____

Deep Listening

_____

_____

_____

Staying

_____

_____

_____

Honesty

_____

_____

_____

Gentleness

_____

_____

_____

New Truth Breakthrough

_____

_____

_____

Journal Entry

Date : _____   Time : _____

Stillness

_____
_____
_____

Release

_____
_____
_____

Deep Listening

_____
_____
_____

Staying

_____
_____
_____

Honesty

_____
_____
_____

Gentleness

_____
_____
_____

New Truth Breakthrough

_____
_____
_____

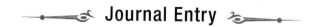# Journal Entry

Date : _____   Time : _____

Stillness

_____

_____

_____

Release

_____

_____

_____

Deep Listening

_____

_____

_____

Staying

_____

_____

_____

Honesty

_____

_____

_____

Gentleness

_____

_____

_____

New Truth Breakthrough

_____

_____

_____

Journal Entry

Date : _____   Time : _____

Stillness

_____

_____

_____

Release

_____

_____

_____

Deep Listening

_____

_____

_____

Staying

_____

_____

_____

Honesty

_____

_____

_____

Gentleness

_____

_____

_____

New Truth Breakthrough

_____

_____

_____

Journal Entry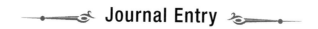

Date : _____   Time : _____

Stillness

_____

_____

_____

Release

_____

_____

_____

Deep Listening

_____

_____

_____

Staying

_____

_____

_____

Honesty

_____

_____

_____

Gentleness

_____

_____

_____

New Truth Breakthrough

_____

_____

_____

Journal Entry

Date : _____   Time : _____

Stillness

_____

_____

_____

Release

_____

_____

_____

Deep Listening

_____

_____

_____

Staying

_____

_____

_____

Honesty

_____

_____

_____

Gentleness

_____

_____

_____

New Truth Breakthrough

_____

_____

_____

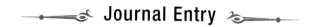# Journal Entry

Date : _____   Time : _____

Stillness

_____
_____
_____

Release

_____
_____
_____

Deep Listening

_____
_____
_____

Staying

_____
_____
_____

Honesty

_____
_____
_____

Gentleness

_____
_____
_____

New Truth Breakthrough

_____
_____
_____

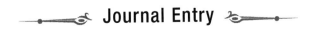 Journal Entry

Date : _____   Time : _____

Stillness

_____
_____
_____

Release

_____
_____
_____

Deep Listening

_____
_____
_____

Staying

_____
_____
_____

Honesty

_____
_____
_____

Gentleness

_____
_____
_____

New Truth Breakthrough

_____
_____
_____

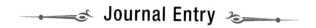 Journal Entry

Date : _____   Time : _____

Stillness

_____

_____

_____

Release

_____

_____

_____

Deep Listening

_____

_____

_____

Staying

_____

_____

_____

Honesty

_____

_____

_____

Gentleness

_____

_____

_____

New Truth Breakthrough

_____

_____

_____

Journal Entry

Date : _____   Time : _____

Stillness

_____

_____

_____

Release

_____

_____

_____

Deep Listening

_____

_____

_____

Staying

_____

_____

_____

Honesty

_____

_____

_____

Gentleness

_____

_____

_____

New Truth Breakthrough

_____

_____

_____

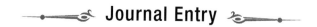 Journal Entry

Date : _____   Time : _____

Stillness

_____

_____

_____

Release

_____

_____

_____

Deep Listening

_____

_____

_____

Staying

_____

_____

_____

Honesty

_____

_____

_____

Gentleness

_____

_____

_____

New Truth Breakthrough

_____

_____

_____

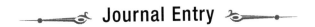 Journal Entry

Date : _____   Time : _____

Stillness

_____

_____

_____

Release

_____

_____

_____

Deep Listening

_____

_____

_____

Staying

_____

_____

_____

Honesty

_____

_____

_____

Gentleness

_____

_____

_____

New Truth Breakthrough

_____

_____

_____

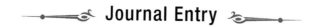# Journal Entry

Date : _____   Time : _____

Stillness

_____

_____

_____

Release

_____

_____

_____

Deep Listening

_____

_____

_____

Staying

_____

_____

_____

Honesty

_____

_____

_____

Gentleness

_____

_____

_____

New Truth Breakthrough

_____

_____

_____

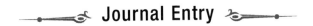 **Journal Entry**

Date : _____   Time : _____

Stillness

_____
_____
_____

Release

_____
_____
_____

Deep Listening

_____
_____
_____

Staying

_____
_____
_____

Honesty

_____
_____
_____

Gentleness

_____
_____
_____

New Truth Breakthrough

_____
_____
_____

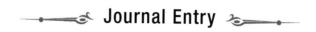

Journal Entry

Date : _____   Time : _____

Stillness

_____

_____

_____

Release

_____

_____

_____

Deep Listening

_____

_____

_____

Staying

_____

_____

_____

Honesty

_____

_____

_____

Gentleness

_____

_____

_____

New Truth Breakthrough

_____

_____

_____

Journal Entry

Date : _____   Time : _____

Stillness

_____
_____
_____

Release

_____
_____
_____

Deep Listening

_____
_____
_____

Staying

_____
_____
_____

Honesty

_____
_____
_____

Gentleness

_____
_____

New Truth Breakthrough

_____
_____
_____

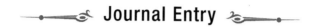# Journal Entry

Date : _____   Time : _____

Stillness

_____

_____

_____

Release

_____

_____

_____

Deep Listening

_____

_____

_____

Staying

_____

_____

_____

Honesty

_____

_____

_____

Gentleness

_____

_____

_____

New Truth Breakthrough

_____

_____

_____

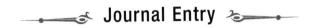# Journal Entry

Date : _____   Time : _____

Stillness

_____

_____

_____

Release

_____

_____

_____

Deep Listening

_____

_____

_____

Staying

_____

_____

_____

Honesty

_____

_____

_____

Gentleness

_____

_____

_____

New Truth Breakthrough

_____

_____

_____

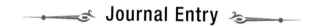 Journal Entry

Date : _____   Time : _____

Stillness

_____
_____
_____

Release

_____
_____
_____

Deep Listening

_____
_____
_____

Staying

_____
_____
_____

Honesty

_____
_____
_____

Gentleness

_____
_____
_____

New Truth Breakthrough

_____
_____
_____

Journal Entry

Date : _____   Time : _____

Stillness

_____

_____

_____

Release

_____

_____

_____

Deep Listening

_____

_____

_____

Staying

_____

_____

_____

Honesty

_____

_____

_____

Gentleness

_____

_____

_____

New Truth Breakthrough

_____

_____

_____

Journal Entry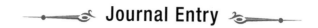

Date : _____   Time : _____

Stillness

_____

_____

_____

Release

_____

_____

_____

Deep Listening

_____

_____

_____

Staying

_____

_____

_____

Honesty

_____

_____

_____

Gentleness

_____

_____

_____

New Truth Breakthrough

_____

_____

_____

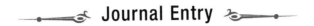 Journal Entry

Date : _____   Time : _____

Stillness

_____

_____

_____

Release

_____

_____

_____

Deep Listening

_____

_____

_____

Staying

_____

_____

_____

Honesty

_____

_____

_____

Gentleness

_____

_____

_____

New Truth Breakthrough

_____

_____

_____

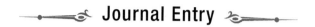

Journal Entry

Date : _____   Time : _____

Stillness

_____
_____
_____

Release

_____
_____
_____

Deep Listening

_____
_____
_____

Staying

_____
_____
_____

Honesty

_____
_____
_____

Gentleness

_____
_____
_____

New Truth Breakthrough

_____
_____
_____

Journal Entry

Date : _____   Time : _____

Stillness

_____

_____

_____

Release

_____

_____

_____

Deep Listening

_____

_____

_____

Staying

_____

_____

_____

Honesty

_____

_____

_____

Gentleness

_____

_____

_____

New Truth Breakthrough

_____

_____

_____

Journal Entry

Date : _____   Time : _____

Stillness

_____

_____

_____

Release

_____

_____

_____

Deep Listening

_____

_____

_____

Staying

_____

_____

_____

Honesty

_____

_____

_____

Gentleness

_____

_____

_____

New Truth Breakthrough

_____

_____

_____

Journal Entry

Date : _____   Time : _____

Stillness

_____

_____

_____

Release

_____

_____

_____

Deep Listening

_____

_____

_____

Staying

_____

_____

_____

Honesty

_____

_____

_____

Gentleness

_____

_____

_____

New Truth Breakthrough

_____

_____

_____

Journal Entry

Date : _____ Time : _____

Stillness

_____

_____

_____

Release

_____

_____

_____

Deep Listening

_____

_____

_____

Staying

_____

_____

_____

Honesty

_____

_____

_____

Gentleness

_____

_____

_____

New Truth Breakthrough

_____

_____

_____

Journal Entry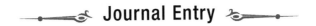

Date : _____   Time : _____

Stillness

_____

_____

_____

Release

_____

_____

_____

Deep Listening

_____

_____

_____

Staying

_____

_____

_____

Honesty

_____

_____

_____

Gentleness

_____

_____

_____

New Truth Breakthrough

_____

_____

_____

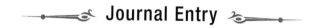 Journal Entry

Date : _____   Time : _____

Stillness

_____

_____

_____

Release

_____

_____

_____

Deep Listening

_____

_____

_____

Staying

_____

_____

_____

Honesty

_____

_____

_____

Gentleness

_____

_____

_____

New Truth Breakthrough

_____

_____

_____

Journal Entry

Date : _____   Time : _____

Stillness

_____

_____

_____

Release

_____

_____

_____

Deep Listening

_____

_____

_____

Staying

_____

_____

_____

Honesty

_____

_____

_____

Gentleness

_____

_____

_____

New Truth Breakthrough

_____

_____

_____

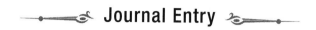

Journal Entry

Date : _____   Time : _____

Stillness

_____
_____
_____

Release

_____
_____
_____

Deep Listening

_____
_____
_____

Staying

_____
_____
_____

Honesty

_____
_____
_____

Gentleness

_____
_____
_____

New Truth Breakthrough

_____
_____
_____

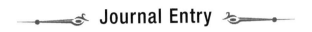# Journal Entry

Date : _____   Time : _____

Stillness

_____

_____

_____

Release

_____

_____

_____

Deep Listening

_____

_____

_____

Staying

_____

_____

_____

Honesty

_____

_____

_____

Gentleness

_____

_____

_____

New Truth Breakthrough

_____

_____

_____

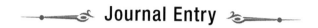# Journal Entry

Date : _____ Time : _____

Stillness

_____

_____

_____

Release

_____

_____

_____

Deep Listening

_____

_____

_____

Staying

_____

_____

_____

Honesty

_____

_____

_____

Gentleness

_____

_____

_____

New Truth Breakthrough

_____

_____

_____

Journal Entry

Date : _____   Time : _____

Stillness

_____

_____

_____

Release

_____

_____

_____

Deep Listening

_____

_____

_____

Staying

_____

_____

_____

Honesty

_____

_____

_____

Gentleness

_____

_____

_____

New Truth Breakthrough

_____

_____

_____

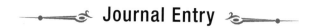# Journal Entry

Date : _____   Time : _____

Stillness

_____
_____
_____

Release

_____
_____
_____

Deep Listening

_____
_____
_____

Staying

_____
_____
_____

Honesty

_____
_____
_____

Gentleness

_____
_____
_____

New Truth Breakthrough

_____
_____
_____

⸻⸺ Journal Entry ⸻⸺

Date : _____   Time : _____

Stillness

_____
_____
_____

Release

_____
_____
_____

Deep Listening

_____
_____
_____

Staying

_____
_____
_____

Honesty

_____
_____
_____

Gentleness

_____
_____
_____

New Truth Breakthrough

_____
_____
_____

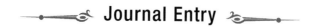 Journal Entry

Date : _____   Time : _____

Stillness

_____

_____

_____

Release

_____

_____

_____

Deep Listening

_____

_____

_____

Staying

_____

_____

_____

Honesty

_____

_____

_____

Gentleness

_____

_____

_____

New Truth Breakthrough

_____

_____

_____